# 100 facts

# Penguins

# 100 facts
# Penguins

Camilla de la Bedoyere

Consultant: Steve Parker

Miles Kelly

First published in 2007 by Miles Kelly Publishing Ltd
Harding's Barn, Bardfield End Green, Thaxted, Essex, CM6 3PX

Copyright © Miles Kelly Publishing Ltd 2007

This edition published 2013

6 8 10 9 7

**Publishing Director:** Belinda Gallagher
**Creative Director:** Jo Cowan
**Editor:** Rosalind McGuire
**Editorial Assistant:** Carly Blake
**Volume Designer:** Sophie Pelham
**Image Manager:** Lorraine King
**Indexer:** Hilary Bird
**Production Manager:** Elizabeth Collins
**Reprographics:** Anthony Cambray, Stephan Davis,
Liberty Newton, Ian Paulyn
**Archive Manager:** Jennifer Hunt
**Assets:** Lorraine King

ISBN 978-1-84810-103-6

Printed in China

British Library Cataloguing-in-Publication Data
A catalogue record for this book is available from the British Library

**ACKNOWLEDGEMENTS**
The publishers would like to thank the following artists who have contributed to this book:
Martin Camm, Annapoala Del Nevo, Gian Paolo Faleshini,
Mike Foster, Ian Jackson, Andrea Morandi, Mike Saunders

All other artworks from the Miles Kelly Artwork Bank

The publishers would like to thank the following sources for the use of their photographs:
Cover Frans Lanting/FLPA; Page 8 Grigory Kubatyan/Fotolia.com; 10 Photolibrary Group Ltd;
14 Elenathewise/Fotolia.com; 16 David Hosking/FLPA; 17 Photolibrary Group Ltd; 19 Photolibrary Group Ltd;
20 Martin Will/Fotolia.com; 21 Andy Rouse/Corbis; 22 Gordan Court/Hedghog House/Minden Pictures/FLPA;
23 Photolibrary Group Ltd; 24 Frans Lanting/Minden Pictures/FLPA; 26 Photolibrary Group Ltd;
31 Kevin Schafer/Corbis; 39 Roger Tidman/FLPA; 43 jbaram/Fotolia.com; 45(t) Ingrid Visser/Foto Natura/FLPA;
45(b) Fred Bavendam/Minden Pictures/FLPA; 47 Martin Harvey; Gallo Images/Corbis

All other photographs are from:
Corel, digitalSTOCK, digitalvision, iStockphoto.com, John Foxx, PhotoAlto,
PhotoDisc, PhotoEssentials, PhotoPro, Stockbyte

Every effort has been made to acknowledge the source and copyright holder of each picture.
Miles Kelly Publishing apologises for any unintentional errors or omissions.

Made with paper from a sustainable forest

www.mileskelly.net
info@mileskelly.net

# Contents

# Bold, beautiful birds

**1** **Penguins are peculiar birds unlike any others on the planet.** They have feathers that are more like fur, and wings that are more like flippers. Penguins live in some of the coldest, windiest and emptiest locations, yet they are still some of the most recognizable birds on Earth.

▶ Penguins, such as these King penguins, are fascinating flightless birds that live extraordinary lives. They are unlike any other type of animal in appearance, and they face incredible challenges to survive from day to day.

# What is a penguin?

**2** **Like all birds, penguins are covered in feathers and lay eggs.** Most birds have bodies that help them fly, but penguins' bodies are perfectly suited to swimming. There are 17 types of penguin, all quite similar in appearance.

**3** **Penguins have stout, upright bodies covered in black-and-white feathers.** Their black backs and white bellies help to camouflage the birds as they swim. When seen from below penguins appear white, blending into the light sky, but when seen from above they blend into the dark sea water.

▶ Birds, like this Chinstrap penguin, are vertebrates – just like reptiles, amphibians and mammals. This means that they have bony skeletons that support their bodies.

Skull

Bill (beak)

Spine

The bones in a penguin's flipper are similar to those in other birds' wings, and a human's arm

Ribcage

Hip bone

Penguins have sharp-clawed toes on their feet

## I DON'T BELIEVE IT!

No one knows for sure where penguins got their strange name from, but it may come from the Latin word for 'fat', which is 'pinguis'.

◄ Penguins evolved (gradually changed over millions of years) from flying birds into flightless birds, so their flippers look quite similar to wings.

**6** **All birds have wings, but not all of them can fly.** Wings are limbs, just like arms and legs, but they are mostly used for flying. The wings of penguins are too small and stumpy to be used for flight, but they have evolved for moving through water.

Flipper of a Magellanic penguin

Wing of a herring gull

**4** **The largest penguin that ever lived was almost as tall as a human.** Scientists know this from studying fossil bones of penguins that lived millions of years ago. These bones give us clues about how prehistoric penguins looked and behaved. *Waimanu*, for example, was a small penguin-like bird that lived around 60 million years ago.

▼ The long-extinct *Waimanu* had bird-like wings, rather than flippers, but probably could not fly.

**5** **Male and female penguins usually look alike.** It is very difficult to tell them apart, but the males are often taller and slightly heavier. Most penguins build nests or dig burrows where they lay their eggs, and both parents help to take care of the eggs and chicks.

# Creature features

**7** **The body of a penguin is perfectly suited to life in the water, rather than life in the air.** The ancestors of penguins were probably flying birds, but at some point in the past their bodies evolved to make them swim faster and better, and they lost their flight feathers. They dive into water to catch sea animals such as fish, so penguins can eat food that few other birds can reach.

▼ Most birds have hollow bones so they can fly. Penguins, such as this Galapagos penguin, have solid bones so they can dive underwater without floating to the surface.

**8** **Penguins are the only flightless waterbirds.** Other flightless birds, such as ostriches, emus and rheas are fast runners on land. They are far too heavy to fly, but can outrun most of their predators. Like penguins, they make their nests on the ground rather than in trees.

## Flying away

Penguins can't fly, but there are plenty of other unusual animals that can soar through the air. Do some research, and find out information on:

1. Flying lemurs
2. Flying squirrels
3. Flying lizards
4. Flying fish

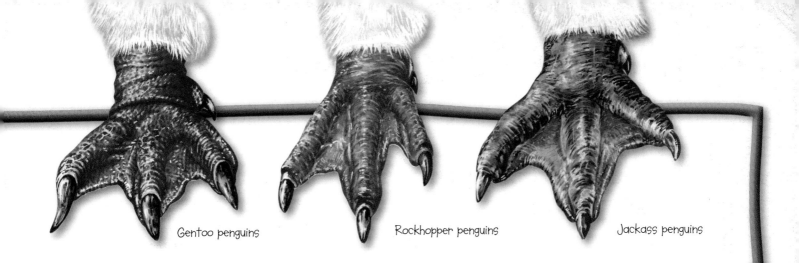

Gentoo penguins

Rockhopper penguins

Jackass penguins

▲ Penguins have webbed feet that help them propel (push) themselves through water. Most penguins have three toes pointing forward, and one pointing backwards. Each toe has a tough claw at the end, to help the penguin keep its grip on rocks and ice.

**9** Penguins may waddle, but they can swim and dive incredibly well, and even on land they are able to get about easily. Penguins that live in snow and ice-covered areas can skid and slide on their bellies across land.

Royal penguin

**10** At first glance, all penguins may look quite similar, but a closer look reveals many differences. The patterns of black-and-white feathers on their bodies vary, and while some penguins have stumpy bills, others have long, slender ones. Some have tufts of brightly coloured feathers on their heads.

King penguin

**11** They may have plump bodies and short legs, but penguins can walk at a fast pace. They scuttle across rocks and ice at about 6 kilometres an hour, which is the same speed as humans walk. They can even climb and jump onto rocks by hauling themselves up using their strong bills and sharp claws.

▶ Penguins have basic similarities, but many are easily recognized by their markings, which are often most obvious on their heads and necks.

Adelie penguin

# On the ice

**12** **Penguins live in the Southern Hemisphere.** This is the half of the Earth below the Equator (the imaginary line that runs through the middle of the Earth). Antarctica and the South Pole are found here, and many types of penguin make this icy habitat their home.

**13** **In the Antarctic, winter temperatures drop as low as −70°C.** The land is covered in ice, and penguins that live here battle against the worst weather on Earth.

**14** **It is easier to stay warm if you have a bigger body.** For this reason, the biggest penguins normally live in the coldest regions, and the smallest penguins live in warmer places.

▼ These eight species (types) of penguin live in or around the freezing Antarctic – the coldest, driest and windiest place on Earth.

King

Adelie

Rockhopper

**15** **The largest penguins are Emperor penguins.** They measure just over one metre in height, and weigh up to 40 kilograms. Their bulk helps them to keep warm in temperatures that reach far below zero.

Emperor

▶ The shaded areas on the map show where these penguins may be found.

SOUTH AMERICA

ATLANTIC OCEAN

AFRICA

INDIAN OCEAN

PACIFIC OCEAN

ANTARC

NEW ZEALAND

AUSTRALIA

**16** **There is a layer of ice 4 kilometres deep covering the Antarctic, and it is so cold even the sea freezes over.** During the winter there may only be sunlight for an hour a day, but in the middle of summer daylight lasts for nearly 24 hours.

Gentoo

Royal

Chinstrap

Macaroni

# Getting warmer

**17** Not all penguins are found in cold places – some live in areas where the weather can be very hot. These birds are found in places such as South America, Australia, New Zealand and South Africa, or even on islands at the Equator, where the temperatures can soar.

**18** Penguins that live in warm places often get too hot. Some of them have patches of bare skin on their faces to help them stay cool. If they get too hot, they may rest in burrows, or leap into the sea.

**19** The air may be warm, but the sea is still cold. Currents from the Antarctic bring chilly water to the coastal areas where these penguins hunt for fish and other food. They have to be able to survive both hot and cold temperatures.

Peruvian

Snares

Little

Fjordland

Magellanic

**20** Most penguins live in remote places where there are few other animals. They are not used to defending themselves against predators such as wild dogs and cats, so they find it difficult to survive anywhere these animals live.

**21** Little penguins of Australia and New Zealand often live near people's homes along the shore. They are shy birds, but often build their nests beneath beach houses. These are the smallest penguins, measuring only 35 centimetres in height.

SOUTH AMERICA
AFRICA
ATLANTIC OCEAN
INDIAN OCEAN
PACIFIC OCEAN
ANTARCTICA
NEW ZEALAND
AUSTRALIA

▲▼ These nine species of penguin, live in the Southern Hemisphere, some distance from the ice-covered South Pole. The shaded areas on the map show where these penguins live.

Erect-crested

Jackass

Galapagos

Yellow-eyed

# Life below zero

**22** **Animals that live in icy places have bodies that can keep heat in and cold out.** Penguins that live in, or near, Antarctica have feathers that lie close to their bodies when they are in the sea, locking out water. When on land, the feathers trap warm air close to the penguins' bodies. On warm days, penguins ruffle their feathers so that warm air escapes.

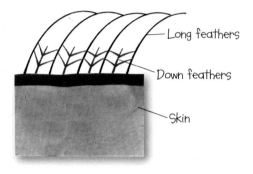

1. Long feathers overlap, trapping warm air next to the skin

Long feathers
Down feathers
Skin

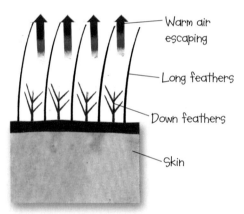

2. Long feathers separate, letting warm air escape

Warm air escaping
Long feathers
Down feathers
Skin

▲ A layer of short feathers lie next to a penguin's skin. The longer top feathers overlap to trap warm air, or separate to allow it to escape.

**23** **Penguins make an oily substance in a special place near their tails.** They spread this over their feathers with their bills and this helps to keep water away from their skin. When penguins clean the dirt from their feathers and coat them with oil they are said to be 'preening'.

◄ This King penguin is using oil from the gland at the base of its tail to preen its feathers.

▶ Emperor penguin chicks sit on their parents' feet to keep from freezing to death on the snow-covered ground.

**24** **A thick layer of fat (blubber), keeps penguins warm.** The blubber may be several centimetres thick. Other animals that live in the oceans, such as whales, also have blubber under their skin. Substances that keep in the warmth, such as blubber, are called 'insulators'.

**25** **Penguins sometimes sunbathe to help warm up their bodies.** The black feathers on their backs absorb sunlight and pass the heat to the penguins' skin. Penguins that live in the Antarctic can even get too hot, and have to take a dip in the sea to cool down!

**26** **Penguin chicks can easily freeze to death.** Parent birds stay with their chicks while they are young, and hold them next to their bodies. This is called brooding and it means that the warmth from the body of the parent is passed to the chick, keeping it warm and dry until it grows its own waterproof feathers.

### I DON'T BELIEVE IT!

Few fish-eating animals live around the Antarctic, so there is plenty of food for those animals, such as penguins, that can cope with extreme temperatures and winds.

# Swimmers and divers

▼ As it swims, the Chinstrap's head, body, legs and tail all make one smooth shape, which glides easily through the water.

**27** Penguins may look clumsy on land, but they move gracefully through the oceans. While other water birds, such as ducks and geese, swim on the top of water, penguins can dive deep below the surface as they hunt for food. Some penguins can swim at speeds of 14 kilometres an hour for short periods of time.

**28** Animals that move through water at speed have bodies that are shaped like bullets. This body shape is said to be 'streamlined' – meaning that it can move smoothly through water. Whales, dolphins, fish and seals also have streamlined bodies.

**29** Fish breathe underwater, but penguins need to come to the surface for air. This means that, no matter how deep or far they swim, they need to put their heads above water to breathe. Some penguins can only stay underwater for a minute or two, but Emperor penguins can dive for 18 minutes at a time and can swim to depths of over 500 metres.

▶ Emperor penguins have highly streamlined bodies and excellent underwater vision, allowing them to dive to incredible depths when they hunt.

**30** Penguins use their flippers to move through water, and their webbed feet to change direction. When penguins swim on the surface of water they use their flippers like oars.

▲ It takes a lot of strength and power for an Emperor penguin to push its large body out of the water and leap on to land.

**31** Swimming penguins leap out of water for a few metres, before diving back in. This is called 'porpoising' (after porpoises, which do this frequently) and it means a penguin can grab a lungful of air without slowing down. This is especially useful when chasing prey, or trying to escape a predator.

## I DON'T BELIEVE IT!

Penguins have excellent vision and can swim to depths where there is little or no light. It's possible that penguins also use other senses to find prey in the dark, but no one knows for sure.

# King penguins

▼ Adult King penguins breed on the rocky islands in and around the Antarctic.

**32** King penguins are unusually colourful, with bold orange and gold patches of plumage. They are the second largest type of penguin, reaching about 90 centimetres in height. Kings live on islands in the Southern Hemisphere, near the fringes of the Antarctic region. When on land, they have to cope with cold, windy weather.

**33** When it is time to breed, King penguins settle on flat land close to the sea. They don't make nests, and the females lay just one egg each year, which is unusual for penguins. The males protect the eggs by holding them on their feet, tucked under the warm fur on their bellies. Keeping the eggs off the ground prevents them from freezing.

**34** Living in a group helps penguins keep warm. Huge groups (colonies) of King penguins huddle together at breeding time. There may be as many as 10,000 birds in a single huddle.

**35** Chicks stay with their parents for about a year before they are ready to survive on their own. Chicks rely on their parents to bring them food, and some chicks have been known to survive for several months without eating.

**36** King penguins mostly eat squid and lanternfish. Lanternfish have an unusual ability to make light in their bodies. The bright flashes of light help the shoal, or group, of lanternfish stick together as they swim through the dark ocean depths, but it also helps King penguins find them too.

▲ Chicks have lots of body fat to keep them warm and provide them with energy while they are waiting for food from their parents. The fat is turned into sugar inside their bodies, and this keeps them alive.

▶ King penguin chicks are covered in downy feathers until they are about 10 months old, when they grow adult feathers. The downy feathers fall out, or moult, as the new plumage grows.

I DON'T BELIEVE IT!

Penguins can take a nap at almost any time, anywhere. They mostly sleep at night, but can doze sitting, standing, lying down or even while swimming.

# Adelie penguins

**37** Adelie penguins are plain-looking birds. They have black coats, white bellies and black heads with white rings around their eyes. Their pointed tails drag behind them as they walk across the Antarctic snow and ice.

▼ Like their close relatives, the Gentoo and Chinstrap penguins, Adelies have long tail feathers that brush the snow as they walk.

▼ Adult Adelies are about 70 centimetres tall and weigh around 5.5 kilograms. They are small, but they are strong swimmers and leapers.

**38** Adelies live in one of the harshest places on Earth, but they are great survivors. Around five million adult Adelies live in the Antarctic, often in huge groups that number tens of thousands.

**39** Pebbles are very valuable to an Adelie penguin. They use them to make their nests, which may also contain bones and moss. Fights often break out over pebbles, with neighbours often stealing the best ones!

**40** A female lays two eggs, and then leaves to hunt in the sea. The male guards the eggs and keeps them warm. If he leaves them they will freeze and the growing chick will die. When the female returns, 10 to 14 days later, the parents take turns to guard the eggs.

▲ Large seabirds will sometimes try to steal food from adult Adelies as they are feeding their chicks.

### I DON'T BELIEVE IT!

Adelie penguin parents sometimes have to travel up to 120 kilometres in search of food to feed their chicks.

**41** Parades of Adelie penguins march towards the edge of the ice. They have to walk from the colony, where their nests are, to the sea, where they can catch food. Once at the water's edge they look out for predators, such as leopard seals, before leaping into the water.

# Life in a rookery

**42** Penguins are sociable animals and they like to live in large groups. They come together, often in their thousands, when it is time to breed. The large groups they form are called rookeries.

▶ A rookery only contains one type, or species, of penguin. These are King penguins. Rookeries are made up of lots of families that are related to one another.

**43** Different types of penguin live in rookeries at different times of year — it all depends on when they breed. Little penguins come ashore in May or June to start mating. They may produce one, two or even three broods (clutches of eggs) through the breeding season. King penguins make their rookeries in October and November.

**44** The largest rookeries may have several million penguins in them. Penguins stay in their rookery during the whole breeding season, leaving only to look for food. For this reason, most rookeries occur in coastal areas, near water. When looking for food, they often stay in small groups and hunt together.

**45** Living in groups helps penguins to stay warm and safe. When the wind blows and the temperature drops far below zero, penguins huddle together for warmth. Huddling also helps to protect the eggs and chicks from predators, especially gulls and other sea birds.

**46** Rookeries are noisy, busy, smelly places. Thousands, or millions, of penguins call to each other constantly. Their waste (called guano) builds up, and some penguins use it as a building material when constructing their nests.

# Emperors

**47** The biggest species (type) of penguin is the Emperor. Along with Kings, they are known as the 'great penguins' and are probably most closely related to the prehistoric giant penguins. They feed mainly on squid, fish and krill – small marine animals similar to shrimps.

▼ Webbed feet and flippers help penguins, such as these emperors, keep their balance on slippery ice, but it's not unusual for them to topple over and start tobogganing on their fronts!

**48** All Emperors live and breed in the Antarctic. Their bodies are adapted for the incredibly cold weather, and they have feathers on their legs all the way down to their feet. There are about 40 breeding colonies of Emperors in the Antarctic, and each colony can have more than 100,000 adults.

**49** When these penguins breed they have to face an extraordinary test of strength and endurance. In March the adults come ashore and walk for up to 200 kilometres to reach their breeding ground. The female lays a single egg, which the male immediately scoops on to his feet, where it is kept warm and safe by a thick flap of skin on his belly.

**50** While the females walk all the way back to the sea to hunt for food, the males huddle together and look after their eggs. They have to wait for nine weeks until the females return – and during this time they survive without any food at all. While the males are waiting they have to cope with hurricane-force winds and some of the coldest temperatures on Earth.

**51** On their return, the females take over the care of the chicks, and the males return to the sea to hunt. The females regurgitate food (bring food back up into their mouths) to feed the chicks. Through the rest of the winter the parents take it in turns to keep the growing chick warm and fetch food from the sea.

### I DON'T BELIEVE IT!

A male Emperor penguin goes without food for up to 115 days while it courts, mates, incubates its egg and looks after its chick. During this time it can lose up to one-third of its body weight.

▲ Chicks are ready to live independently by summer time. Their parents do not teach them how to swim, dive or hunt – they just know instinctively how to do these things.

# Say and display

**52** All animals communicate with each other, and voices and body language are two of the most important ways. Penguins often communicate by calling to each other. The type of calls depend on the species of penguin, and what message they want to get across.

**53** Penguins use body language to choose a mate. When males want to attract a female they stand tall with their necks outstretched, bray loudly and spread their flippers wide. Interested females copy the males and raise their heads, stretching tall.

◀ Chinstrap penguins put on a display to impress potential mates. They bob their heads up and down and make a great deal of noise, sounding like braying donkeys or hissing cats.

## QUIZ

Which of the examples of body language listed below will a penguin use to attract a mate?

1. Standing tall
2. Spreading their flippers wide
3. Making loud braying noises

Answer:
All are true.

◀ Male Gentoo penguins offer their females pebbles for building a large nest, which will protect their two eggs.

**54** When an adult penguin returns from the sea it can't rely on sight alone to find its chick. Penguins sometimes have their own 'meeting places' where members of the family go to find one another. Adults can recognize the screech of their own chicks, even when thousands of other chicks are calling at the same time.

**55** Adelie penguins defend their territories fiercely. They use body language – such as pointing with their flippers and staring – to scare others away. If their warnings aren't heeded they attack the other animal, beating them with their flippers.

**56** Gentoo penguins value pebbles, which they use to build their nests. Males sometimes give their mates pebbles as a gift. Penguins steal nesting materials, such as pebbles and plants, from one another's nests and this can cause fights.

▼ Royal penguins often squabble over nesting spaces and these fights can result in eggs being crushed.

29

# Gentoos and Chinstraps

**57** Gentoos have bright—orange bills and feet. Their feathers are black and white, with white patches above their eyes. Gentoos gather in large groups when they nest. They lay two eggs in September or October and the chicks hatch 34 days later. Both parents share the task of feeding the chicks.

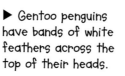

▶ Gentoo penguins have bands of white feathers across the top of their heads.

**58** Adult penguins moult (lose their feathers) when their youngsters become independent. During moulting, which takes place once a year, a penguin sheds its damaged or old feathers so new ones can replace them. A moulting penguin looks strange, as new feathers force the old ones out. Moulting takes several weeks, and during this time an adult penguin can't go into the sea because its plumage is not waterproof.

◀ Moulting adult penguins have to go without food until their new plumage grows. Before moulting, penguins increase the amount they eat to build stores of fat in their bodies.

**59** There are around 12 million Chinstraps. These medium-sized penguins have black-and-white feathers. Chinstraps can be recognized by the distinctive narrow band of black feathers that run from one side of their heads to the other, under their bills. This makes them look as if they are wearing helmets, which are strapped on under their chins, and gives them their name.

**I DON'T BELIEVE IT!**

Chinstraps can be very aggressive, and will beat each other with their stumpy wings or bite hard. They will even attack humans if they come into contact with them.

**60** Chinstraps and Gentoos live near the Antarctic. They swim in freezing water, searching for tiny marine animals and fish to eat. When they come to land they often huddle together on massive ice floes.

# Chilly chicks

**61** Life for a penguin chick is very tough, and many never make it to adulthood. Female penguins normally lay two eggs, but often only one survives. The first chick hatches from its egg several days before the second, and gets a head start. By the time the second chick emerges, the first chick is much bigger and stronger, and is more likely to be fed by its parents.

**62** Young chicks are covered in fluffy feathers, and they look nothing like their parents for some time. The feathers are not good at keeping heat in, but they allow the heat from the body of an adult penguin to get to the chick's skin. Chicks that live in very cold places may easily freeze to death, especially if their parents get so hungry they have to desert them to feed.

**63** Chicks huddle together in groups when their parents leave them. These groups are called nurseries, or crèches, and a few adult penguins usually stay behind to protect the youngsters from predators.

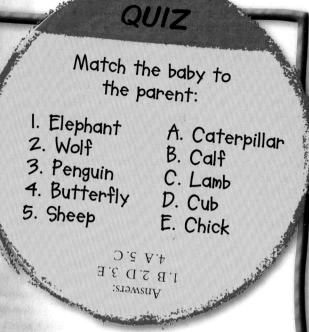
◄ These Emperor chicks are huddling together for warmth.
They rely on their parents until they have grown thicker
layers of waterproof feathers. When they have grown
their first adult plumage, chicks are known as fledglings.

**64** Penguin chicks can
survive for days without food,
unlike the chicks of other birds.
As it gets older, a chick's parents may
disappear for days, or weeks at a
time, hunting for food in the ocean.
Thanks to their thick layers of fat,
penguin chicks do not starve to death
during this time. Birds that fly can't
have large stores of fat, or they would
never get off the ground!

▶ Some penguins, like this Gentoo, lay two
eggs. Only one chick will survive unless the
parents can find enough food for both.

# South American penguins

**65** Some penguins never see snow and can suffer from too much heat! These warm-weather penguins have to shelter from the hot sun, rather than the polar winds of the South Pole. They do not need so many layers of fat to keep them warm, so they are thinner than the penguins of Antarctica.

**66** Almost 500 years ago, an explorer from Portugal came to South America and thought he'd found a new type of flightless goose. The man was called Ferdinand Magellan and he gave his name to these new birds – Magellanic penguins. Sadly Magellan and his crewmates were not very interested in the birds, except as a source of food.

**67** Magellanic penguins live around the coast of South America and nearby islands. When they come to land to breed they choose large, flat, sandy or pebbly places to build their nests and often share their nesting grounds with sea lions. Although the sea lions rarely eat the penguins, they often attack them.

▼ Magellanic penguins lay their eggs in burrows, which they dig near bushes, shrubs or grass so that they can shelter from the wind and sun.

▲ Peruvian penguins lay their eggs in burrows dug out of guano (their waste), which has built up over many centuries.

Galapagos penguins spend a lot of time in the water to keep cool. When on land they hold their flippers over their feet to stop them getting sunburnt!

**68** Galapagos penguins live further north than any other penguins. The make their homes on the Galapagos Islands, which lie off the west coast of South America and cross the Equator. Here the temperatures soar and the sun is very strong. To try and keep cool these little penguins hunt for fish and squid during the day and only come on to land at night.

**69** Peruvian penguins live on the desert coasts of Peru and Chile, in South America. Like Galapagos and Magellanic penguins they make burrows to protect their eggs and chicks, although they sometimes build nests in caves or under rocks. They are very shy birds, and avoid humans.

◄ Peruvian penguins have a thick black bar of feathers across their front. They are sometimes called Humboldts, which is the name of a current of cold water that flows along the South American coast.

# Penguin predators

**70** A predator is an animal that preys on (hunts) other animals to eat. Penguins mainly live in places where there are few predators. When they dive into the ocean, penguins need to stay alert, as there are sea-living predators such as sharks, seals and whales that may hunt them.

**72** Penguin eggs make tasty food for many different animals. Parent birds sometimes have to leave their eggs or chicks unprotected. At these times hungry predators, such as skuas and gulls, will try and grab them.

**73** Penguins on land may be attacked by wild animals. In Antarctica, penguins have little to fear from other animals, as few creatures can survive in this barren habitat. Elsewhere, however, nesting penguins are easy prey for cats, dogs, foxes and ferrets, and if they see one of these predators approaching they head for the water quickly.

**71** Leopard seals and sea lions attack penguins when they swim and dive. These big animals spend most of their lives in water, but come to the surface to breathe. Some of them can stay underwater for more than an hour at a time and can dive to depths of 100 metres. Penguins are the leopard seal's main source of food.

▼ Leopard seals can reach 3 metres in length. They have long, sharp teeth that are perfect for biting into the flesh of penguins, seals and squid.

▲ If they are attacked in the ocean, penguins swim fast to escape, or leap out of the water on to land.

**74** **Mighty killer whales are powerful predators.** They often hunt in groups and may swim right up a beach to catch seals or penguins. They have been known to nudge large ice floes, where penguins are resting, and tip them into the water.

# Jackass penguins

**75** Jackass penguins get their name from their loud, braying call, which sounds like a donkey, or jackass. They are also known as African or Black-footed penguins. Jackass penguins reach about 60 centimetres in height and live on the coasts of South Africa and nearby islands.

**76** Only a few hundred years ago there were millions of Jackass penguins living in South Africa. Now there are only 50,000 breeding pairs. Many have been killed by hunters, or have lost their habitats. Now they are protected, but they remain in danger of extinction (dying out).

▲ Jackass penguins are popular with tourists in South Africa, who enjoy watching these tame and friendly birds.

## TRUE OR FALSE?

1. Emperor penguins live in Australia.
2. Penguins can breathe underwater.
3. Kiwis are also flightless birds.
4. The Antarctic is at the South Pole.

Answers:
3 and 4 are true.

**77** **Jackasses build their burrows in guano.** Huge piles of bird waste covered many coasts and islands for hundreds of years, until Europeans began to remove it to use as fertilizer (a substance that is dug into soil to help plants grow). Without the guano, the penguins couldn't protect their eggs and chicks. Now local people and tourists are giving them ready-made burrows.

▲ While some penguins use pebbles to build their nests, Jackass penguins favour twigs.

**78** **Females lay their eggs throughout the year.** Usually two eggs are laid at a time, and they are cared for by both parents, who may stay together for life. The eggs are incubated (kept warm) for about 40 days before hatching.

**79** **If the weather gets too hot, Jackass penguins leave their nests and return to the cool water.** These hot days sometimes happen at the beginning of a nesting season, when some penguins have already laid their eggs. The parents may not return for six weeks, and by then their eggs will have been eaten by sea birds.

# Dinner time

**80** Penguins are active birds, and they need to eat a lot of food to give them energy. Most penguins survive on a mixed diet of fish, squid and crustaceans, such as crabs and krill. Adelie penguins feed on krill, and can eat up to one kilogram every day.

**81** Penguins have a clever way of providing food for their youngsters. When adult penguins catch food for their chicks they have to carry it – firstly as they swim through the ocean – and then as they walk to their breeding grounds. They do this by means of a special stomach-like pouch, called a crop, in their throats. The food can stay in the crop for several days.

▶ Young penguins, like this Chinstrap chick, peck at an adult's mouth to encourage them to regurgitate their food. Chicks pester any passing adult for food, not just their parents!

## QUIZ

1. How much krill can Adelie penguins eat in a day?
2. What is the name of the stomach—like pouch in a penguin's throat?
3. Do penguins have teeth?

Answers:
1. One kilogram 2. Crop 3. No

**82** Parent birds feed their chicks by regurgitating the food from their crops. Food passes from the parent's crop to its bill, and then into a chick's open mouth. Most penguins live near the sea, so they are never far from food, but Emperor penguins sometimes have to travel over 1000 kilometres in a single hunting trip. They can carry more than 4 kilograms of food in their crops.

**84** Catching hold of a slippery fish is not always easy. Penguins don't have teeth so they swallow their food whole. Their bills have sharp edges that can grip a fish or squid tightly.

**83** Seas and oceans may be teeming with life in some areas, but rather empty in others. This is because the oceans of the world are greatly affected by warm and cold currents of water that flow through them. The currents change during the seasons, and over many years. Places with cool currents often have more food than those with warm currents, so this is where penguins hunt.

▶ Spikes inside their mouths and spines on their tongues help penguins, like this Jackass, keep hold of their prey until they can swallow it.

# Crested clowns

▲ Rockhoppers bounce from boulder to boulder. They are aggressive, noisy birds.

**85** The six species of crested penguins have decorative head feathers. Rockhoppers are one of the most familiar crested penguins, and the smallest. They are found mainly on islands in the subantarctic region where there are no beaches and they have to slip, slide and jump into the water. To get back on land they leap straight out of the sea.

**86** Fjordland penguins of New Zealand are so shy that little is known about them. They hide in their nests at the foot of trees or in sheltered areas of forests where they live. Scientists fear that few of these penguins are left, and they may become extinct.

**87** Snares penguins live only on Snares Islands near New Zealand and their habitat is protected. People are rarely allowed on the islands, which are covered in trees and plants. The penguins make their rookeries in the forests.

▲ Erect-crested penguins are closely related to Snares and Fjordland penguins.

**88** **Crested penguins usually lay two eggs.** Only one is likely to hatch – usually the second one, which is larger. The parents sometimes destroy the first egg, but no one knows why they do this.

**89** **Like all crested penguins, Macaronis have short, red bills.** They are the largest crested penguins, reaching about 60 centimetres in height. Royal penguins look similar, but they have white faces and throats.

**90** **Erect-crested penguins have spiky crests.** Unlike other crested penguins, they can raise and lower their crests. They are sociable birds, and make large rookeries, sometimes alongside Rockhoppers.

▼ Male and female Macaroni penguins take turns to incubate their eggs.

# Penguins and people

**91** Penguins and people have only got to know each other in the last 500 years. Many of the places where penguins live were unknown to people until then. Even New Zealand, a home to many penguins, was not inhabited by people until 1000 years ago, when hunters from Polynesia settled there.

▶ Like all penguins, Snares penguins have to compete with humans for fish in the oceans. They are also affected by pollution in the water.

▶ Great Auks were hunted by people for food, along with their eggs.

**92** The Great Auk is thought to be a relative of penguins, but was hunted to extinction by humans in 1844. Like penguins, Great Auks were flightless diving birds, but they lived in the Arctic, close to the fishing areas of Europeans. If penguins lived in the Arctic it is likely many of them would have been hunted to extinction too.

**93** Three hundred years ago, sailors and fishermen hunted penguins for the fat and oil in their bodies. The oil was used in lamps in the days before electricity, and in manufacturing. In the Falklands Islands alone 2.5 million penguins were killed for their oil in just 16 years.

▼ Today, scientists study penguins, like this Little penguin, to find out the best ways to protect them for the future.

**94** The oceans provide food for humans as well as penguins. Fish are a source of protein for one billion people already, but there will not be enough fish for future generations – of either penguins or people. In some parts of the oceans, local populations of fish have already disappeared.

**95** Penguins are popular animals at zoos and wildlife parks around the world. These places give people a chance to watch and learn about these fascinating creatures, without having to travel to the far corners of the Earth!

# Penguins in peril

**96** Yellow-eyed penguins may become extinct during this century. They live in forests in New Zealand, but many trees have been cut down to build homes and farms. The penguins are attacked by predators that have been brought to the country, such as cats, dogs, foxes and ferrets. There are only about 1500 pairs of Yellow-eyed penguins left in the wild.

**97** Some Adelie penguins have dangerous chemicals in their bodies. These have come from paints, pesticides and other substances that have been dumped in the sea. People have been treating the ocean like a rubbish tip, and the animals and plants that live there are now suffering because of the pollution.

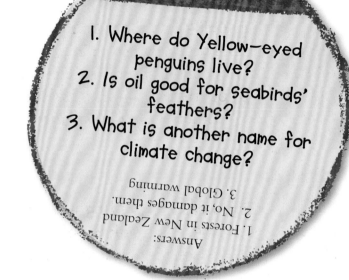

◄ The habitats of the remaining Yellow-eyed penguins are now protected, but their numbers continue to fall.

**98** Oil spills have caused the deaths of many penguins around the world. Huge ships (tankers) carry oil across the oceans. They often leak gallons of oil into the water, suffocating many marine animals. The oil damages the feathers of seabirds, and many of them die.

**99** The world is getting warmer, and this affects penguins. As the air is polluted the weather is changing. This is called global warming – and it will have an impact on habitats all over the world, especially the Antarctic, where the ice is starting to melt.

**100** No one wants to see penguins disappear, but making the world a safer place for them is not an easy task. In the past, people have put the lives of penguins, and many other wild animals, in peril. People today will have to work hard to build a better future for all of the world's wildlife.

▼ Emperor penguins nest on winter ice. If this ice melts early, because of global warming (a change in the Earth's temperature), the species will struggle to survive.

▲ The plumage of this African penguin has been covered in oil that leaked from a tanker. If the penguin tries to clean its feathers, it will be poisoned by the oil.

# Index